Running Late

Running Late

Poems by

Mark Belair

Cover design by Shay Culligan
Cover art by Barbara Amstutz

ISBN: 978-1-950462-26-1

Kelsay Books Inc.

kelsaybooks.com

502 S 1040 E, A119
American Fork, Utah 84003

For Thomas

Acknowledgments

Grateful acknowledgement is made to the editors of the following journals, who first published these poems:

Alabama Literary Review: "the storm," "The Ocean"
Alexandria Quarterly: "In Study"
Apple Valley Review: "The Corner"
Avatar Review: "The Master of Ceremonies"
Bluestem: "Train Station"
Buck Off Magazine: "Clouds"
Burningword Literary Journal: "Mine," "Waiters," "After Loss," "Jingle"
Carbon Culture Review: "The Brace," "Park Bench"
the Cincinnati Review: "The Bus Stop Crush"
Common Ground Review: "The Stranger"
Crack the Spine Literary Magazine: "the rooming house"
Door Is A Jar Magazine: "Born Again"
Evening Street Review: "The Basketball," "River and Leaves," "icons," "setting the watch"
Forge: "Summer Radiator," "Come Silence," "The Trinket," "By the Natural History Museum," "The Wedding Picture," "Bus Driver," "Burials," "Disturbances," "Early Spring," "Sunset"
the Furious Gazelle: "Access Door"
Gemini Magazine: "chick"
GNU Journal: "Ruins"
Green Hills Literary Lantern: "Mounds," "Alleyways"
Iodine Poetry Journal: "Handles"
Juked: "Symptoms"
Mantis: "the hulk"
the Minnesota Review: "the wooden floor"
Pour Vida: "Bag of Blood"
Poydras Review: "Bikes"

the Round: "Donuts"
Sanskrit Literary-Arts Journal: "The Hush," "the notebooks"
Slab: "Across the Park"
Stand Magazine: "Trust," "DJs"
Stickman Review: "Spring Snow"
Streetlight Magazine: "Pecking," "Spring Chill," "The Project"
The Summerset Review: "Strollers"
Tiger's Eye: A Journal of Poetry: "Hipster Hats"
the Tower Journal: "Among Trades," "Solace," "Summer Stoop
        Sitting," "the reunion," "Heat Lightning"
Vending Machine Press: "The Alley," "The Future," "Around
        Town," "Four-Way Independence"
Whistling Shade: "Early Snow"
Zone 3: "Playgroup"

Contents

Running Late Yet Watching Others

Running Late Yet Having To Wade

Running Late Yet Taking the Garden Path

Running Late

Yet Finishing the Work

Handles

In the late day garden shed, in the late summer light,
the old yard tools—rakes, shovels, axes, hoes—form

a lean-to offering a fan of worn wooden handles
that nestle with neither eagerness nor reluctance

but with a simple, calm
grace that seems to glow

in the filtered light, each tool stripped to
its essence, pared to a monk's purity—yet

each as narrowly incomplete as me
until, work to take on, I take hold.

Among Trades

A butcher cradles a baby
about the size of a roast.

He sports a chef's hat
and paunch-tightened apron stained red.

This butcher and his baby—
blood supporting blood—

laughing in the sun
with pagan delight.

*

Alone,
though not terribly.

The advent
of ever-novel landscapes

diverting the development
of an ever-articulated self.

Wind streaming over
the roadie,

smoothing him down,
intricacies gone,

hard core
intact.

*

His disheveled appearance—shirt misbuttoned, glasses crook-
ed, hair a tangle, curly beard untrimmed—broadcasts

how little this professor
considers his body,

how it is not
his arena, how, instead,

the mind is,
a mind obsessed

with a scrupulously groomed
appearance

in word, logic, rigor of thought—
don't challenge him there

unless you have an endowment
to match,

this jock of the mind
negating his body

so as to nakedly
strut his stuff.

*

Steamy summer night
with a wan sliver moon over Lincoln Center,

the all-cab traffic wailing
at the slow pedestrians crossing the street,

the polished musical performances done,
the posh restaurants closing down

(rattan sidewalk café chairs piled-up and chained together),
cab fares—despite the prosperous-looking pedestrians—scarce,

the stuck immigrant drivers—leaning harder and harder
on their horns—a long way from home.

the wooden floor

the cozy / cluttered / coffee and tea import shop / conducts its
workday on a dark / creaky / wooden floor / each slim strip

scarred and stained and cracked from dropped wooden barrels /
spilled drinks / boot-crushed beans / and the weight of waiting
customers and piled-up days / though

the odd plank / free of distress / seems only gently / beautifully
aged

until one day the floor's dream kicks in / or so i dream / the dream
of rolling back up and retiring to the woods / its strips restoring to
rings / its trunk recrusting amid its fellows

while airing a faint / bracing / complex scent of its grinding / yet
enlivening / working life

Running Late

Yet Meandering

Access Door

This once-
shiny metal door
flat to the sidewalk
that admits power company electricians
to runs of buried cables
carries a skim coat
of scum: dirt first, on which grows
moss that catches
fallen twigs and leaves
mashed in by footsteps and rain, the thick coat
muddy and scented
as something obscure
remembered from childhood, something
once experienced
by a wandering six-year-old
mill-town boy
stopped by such a door, its presence
faintly familiar, a door
work-worn and gently yielding—yet
still holding the boy
as he ventured on it, then bounced on it:
a meaningful
but murky experience
that became—if no more clear—
memory-permanent
after he ran home for a baked-bean supper
prepared by his ladling mother
for his extended family
of work-worn, gently yielding,
French Canadian millhands.

Mounds

My maternal grandfather,
who hated shopping and unnecessary noise,
took me shopping when I was one,
me pulling my quacking toy duck.

When I was two, my grandfather
dug a big hole in our yard for an oak sapling,
making me his Official Helper
despite the pleas of the worried women
who, not knowing me as well as did he,
were afraid I'd fall in.

My grandfather, when I was three,
set a pine board on his workbench,
gave me a hammer and roofing nails
(their heads, like mine, childishly large)
and set me to pounding
while he looked on with pride,
bragging to the nervous women that,
just like him, I never missed once.

Before I was four, my grandfather
was dead and I didn't stop pounding nails
into the board until, big heads crowding
up on each other, I'd made rises
that looked like burial mounds.

Then we moved and, in the confusion,
left the board behind.

My mother, once we were settled-in,
wondered aloud what the new owners,
when they saw that board, must have
thought.

24

Probably, she then remarked, *just that some little boy who lived there before could have got hurt doing that.*

Donuts

In the sober Connecticut mill town
of my boyhood, one street ran
slantwise downhill
to the wild degree
that my sister, also in the back seat, would
slide my way and—us both laughing—
slam into me, then
at the leveling place, she'd
scootch back to swing open her door
and charge toward the bakery, its shelves
stacked with Sunday morning donuts—
we'd just come from church.

Powdered sugar and jelly were our
worldly rewards
for having sat service-still during Mass—
though I did have
the absent, scolded habit of licking the polished pew
(my mouth landed right at that height)
beneath my prayer-folded hands.

But that first bite of donut—
coming after our giddy, tilted ride—
was the sacrament
that purged,
for another blessed week,
the waxed-wood taste of church.

the storm

rain so glazed the windshield / that my grandmother couldn't see /
so she pulled off to wait out the storm

the windows steamed up / and the sky further darkened / as we
listened to the violent thunder

just pépère bowling in heaven my grandmother said / to calm me
and my big sister / though neither of us was scared

then a whimpering neared / frightened barking / then claws began
desperately scratching / down the outside of my back door

i cleared my fogged window / and a black dog / yellow teeth
bared / shot at my hand

now i was scared

then my grandmother cried *he'll scratch my door clean of paint /
let him in*

i couldn't do it / so my sister / sensing advantage / reached across
me and the gangly dog / wet and wild / lunged inside / scampered

around our unsatisfactory laps / then settled in the well at my
raised-up feet

each petrified / him of the thunder / me of him / we both panted /
chests working like crazed accordions / as the windy rain

streaked the windows / hammered the roof / rocked the car / the
thunder moving directly overhead

then after one especially nasty clap / our eyes helplessly met / and
the dog / sensing a compatriot in fear / if not its cause / snuffled his

cold / wet snout into my scrunched-up legs / and i / emboldened by
his humble appeal / gingerly patted his head

then he licked my hand and / though that was gross / we both
began to breathe again

when the storm at last subsided / and pépère / and his dark
bowling / grew remote / i opened my door and the dog

jumped out and trotted off / *poor thing* my grandmother said as she
started the car

then we drove off / windows clearing / the sun / breaking through
the clouds / surprisingly warm

The Basketball

My first basketball—
a growing-boy gift for my sixth birthday—
my mother marked on alternate panels with our name,

so that if lost or stolen
it could be claimed, a gesture that shamed me—
and fit her suspicious nature—with its caution and lack of trust.

But lost it became—
vindicating her—after a game in the park.
Then a few days later, a four-year-old showed

up at the court
bouncing a basketball
with its alternate panels blacked out.

That's mine, I said.
No it ain't, the little guy replied.
You covered over my name, I insisted.

No I didn't, he said,
clutching the ball to his chest,
My mom decorated this and it's mine!

His because he stole it.
Decorated so he could use it.
His mom an accomplice to his crime.

A mom who was
poor and mean and, though she
cursed him constantly, wanted him to have.

I told my mom and
she told me to steal it back.

But he guarded it
well and he was too little—

despite the suspicions
aimed at me

by my mother—
to hit.

the hulk

our downstairs neighbor nat / a good / hardworking family man /
had an old nash that / when he tried to start it one morning / caught
fire and burned outside our second-story window / leaving a
blackened hulk that drew curious neighbors who / arms folded in
judgment / frowned and shook their sage heads

it seemed unfair / this private misfortune compounded by
occurring as a public display

and as i / a boy witnessing his first fire and aftermath / stared down
from our window / it came to seem that nat's car / with its dandy
two-tone paint job and woven-plastic upholstery / features that
reminded me of nat himself / who sported a trim moustache /
polka-dot bow tie / and straw hat / was not so much destroyed / as
undisguised / its dark / hidden soul / made manifest

and even after it was towed away / when i looked down / the hulk
was there

Running Late

Yet Held in Place

Summer Radiator

The cloud-softened summer sun
bathes an old black radiator, one
cool to the touch, its heat
on hiatus, each
arched, filigreed radiant
in the round-shouldered attention
of choristers in a cast-iron choir, a choir
holding silent
until fall, one night, arrives
with the chill
of a strict choirmaster
to conduct its conduction
back to blasting, soul-warming life.

The Brace

An old stone church, collapsing wall
braced, the construction pit next to it

reeking of dirt in the rain, its crippled
state engendered by nothing dramatic—

no earthquakes, no hurricanes—just
the wear of ordinary weather, erosion

that occasioned a soft, slow shifting
in a deep, hidden, foundational place

into which the builders long ago
put their faith.

Bikes

Through the open door
of the closed pizza parlor

glint three delivery bikes
parked in a line in the dark,

the immigrant deliverymen
due soon

after having worked
late in the rain

for tips only
while fielding complaints

in a language
not their own, later

sleeping in an illegally
partitioned fire trap—

three cots
parked in a line in the dark.

Hipster Hats

The sidewalk vendor selling summer hipster hats—
narrow-brimmed straw fedoras—
stacks them in tenuous towers
that tilt forward as if filled with
hidden hipster heads
too chill to look up
to the parade of the mundane—the kids, office workers, food
delivery guys, slow-struggling elderly—all of whom—
by being noisy, bland, pressured,
or in overt need—lack for cool.

Then a sly sideways breeze
tips the towers over,
and the hipster hats tumble and land
empty-side up.

Across the Park

Across the broad park, through
winter-bare trees, stands
a front of old apartment buildings
never my home
so seeming to hold, beyond
each blank window, one
of my unlived lives; a front
of refusing panes
that invite me to peer
back through the dark, dense branches
that shade the open paths
and handmade ways
I just straggled through
to imagine in the imperfect, but only,
way I can—
as who I've become—
those I might have been.

The Master of Ceremonies

The winter wind
gusts from behind me,
fat snowflakes overtaking
my walking pace and twirling on
the pavement ahead like circus artists
flying free of the trapeze and tumbling while
more snowflakes collide in comic crosswinds like clowns
scattering from a swarm of snarling-wild-animal-snow-swirls,
the whole snow circus procession heralding the splendid arrival
of me, the Master of Ceremonies, who enters waving to the
adoring crowd, its snowflake applause covering me head
to foot, a cloak of silliness-appropriated snowflakes
that—as I stamp indoors, remove my boots,
hang up my coat, brew tea, and resume
my responsible routine—melt,
each one, like boys, once
unique, they say.

Solace

A sentimental Mexican ballad
pours from the French café's scratchy sound system:

easy trumpets; strumming guitars;
crisp congas; calmly agitating guiros.

And a solo violin, so yearningly
out of tune with itself

as to play in perfect
tune with me.

Running Late

Yet Keeping Close

River and Leaves

A branch
lush with leaves

hangs over
a silvery river,

its skirt of green
reflecting

the water's
dappled passage

like a screen
for the river's dreams

while the dangling leaves
glimmer

in the water
like a parallel dream,

river and leaves
merged

by this mutual
mirroring—

lovers
dreaming into each other.

The Alley

Its chain-link fence stands
padlocked and topped with
concertina wire while the
metal doors set in the sides
of the buildings that line it
look long bolted shut and the
iron grills that guard those
buildings' windows seem
permanently crusted in rust
that seems also to have spread
like fire down the fire escapes
that tumble past twin floodlights
now busted, floodlights that
once lit the two junked cars
that have sat there for so long
that from around their split tires
sprout tender green shoots, shoots
that also thrive between all the
buckling paving stones that hardened
this century-old alley, this brutalized
relic of possession and abandonment
returning, at last, to its first, gentle love.

The Bus Stop Crush

She untangles a white earbud cord
with knowing fingers

and I feel—as I observe her deftness—
untangled too; then she

angles the buds
into her delicate ears

and I feel—as I observe her care—
made snugly secure; then she

closes her dark eyes
to her selection of music, music

I can't hear
though I can't help but hear—

despite the raucous bus stop crush—
the music of her.

Bag of Blood

I am brimming
with blood.

My skin
taut with it.

My resting hands
pulsing with it.

I'm a bone-borne
bag of blood.

Like an IV, I could be
hung and sourced.

I'm alive with it,
made alive by it.

Circulating it my
animal duty—

my species of
spirituality.

Blood secures me, yet
lets me run

wild—my pounding legs
streaming with it.

My blood-rich heart
what, of me, loves

me most; what, of myself,
I love most.

It is core to all I am.
And beats

quietly at night,
repeating your name.

Telling me, my love,
that if you'll

take such a thing
it's yours.

Ruins

Our subway car, on an elevated track,
whipped past a long-abandoned metal

switching tower—or power sub-station?—
its curled paint stiffened, its outside—

propane?—tanks rusted around, a bird—
a starling?—(we were traveling too fast

to know anything for sure) perched atop
one tank, beak open in a song, it seemed,

of mating masked by our own gruff rumble.
Then our speed swept the moment away

and I closed my eyes to imprint
this version of an ancient yet still

soaring vision—torn, as ever, from
the hard, hurtling commonplace—

of love
among the ruins.

Running Late

Yet Stalling

Come Silence

The caption said the dead man
had been trampled in a crowd.

One boot was gone
and his long-sleeve checkered shirt was torn.

Had he worn his boots and long-sleeve shirt
in case it might turn cold?

Or had he felt, that morning,
rain coming on?

*

The oxygen machine pumped
as it had for months

until his daughter, who an hour before
helped him bear dying—

It's all right to let go, she whispered, crying,
You've done your job—

heard it working and—its duty done—
snapped it off.

Then a hard silence
fell, one

that widened
the one her father,

still in bed,
already inhabited.

53

*

Being here, alone
with the rain

tapping the roof shingles
and streaking the windowpanes

despite your death,
I remember

you once said
this

was what
you believed in.

icons

the ladies at church / parading fine sunday hats / or those out on the
town / for lunch and a show / still pierce him / all reminders / of his
high-spirited mother

soon after her death / he found an insurance policy so old / that his
father / long ago struck and killed while providing roadside help /
was still the beneficiary

and by straightening that out / he first learned / never having seen
his father's death certificate before / of the injuries he sustained /
fractured skull / shattered bones / internal organ lacerations / facts

his mother withheld at the time / as he was only in junior high
school / injuries now so far in the past / their details / he said /
made him feel closer to his father

for grievous as the list was / it was something new about him /
something that gave him more of his father / even if about how he
suffered and died / to love

then he put the old death certificate down / beside his mother's
newest feathered hat / the long years bridging these two icons of
loss / evoking the distance away from him / he knew as he wept

his mother / following his father / was already traveling

The Trinket

So many loners
I have known have
died leaving
few family and friends, deaths
that occurred so long ago
I may be—or soon could become—
the last mortal left
to have witnessed their life,
the sole remainder
from their small, scattered estate,
the final traceable trinket
on a flea market table
sunlit until shadowed
by what will take it away.

Pecking

A pigeon
pecking its tail clean
on a shady tenement fire escape

gives me
pause to feel, in its
twisting instinct, the fact of life

after death—
not an afterlife of mine, but of
its spawning species after my demise,

each bird
in each generation
curled and tucked toward its tail,

each making a
soft, gray, feathery circle
surrounding—as if protecting—

its heart,
its presence
in my lost paradise.

The Hush

The fog
revealed all

the drizzly morning
I first

trolled the beach
in Maine

alone, a boy
in a rubber raincoat

stunned still
by the haunting

hush
from every

shell, for each
once held

something alive,
a being

(I could hear
in the hush)

longing to return,
longing for the stormy sea,

longing for a resurrection
for which they had—

the cold, drifting, obliterating
fog whispered—

no
prayer.

The Stranger

Time was a stranger back then, someone who—
in the course of a long summer afternoon of love
and talk over what we could muster for a meal—

passed at a remove; someone not actually encountered
but merely, casually viewed; someone who, while real,
didn't really concern himself with timeless lovers like us.

Only later did that heavy stranger walk in unannounced,
cast off his black hat and coat and, right at our little table
for two, sit himself down, impatient, hungry, unforgiving.

The Future

Nearing death, it must be difficult to envision the days
we'll never see, the loss too great to contemplate—
yet how else, as we decline, to remain fully alive?

Perhaps the key would be to conjure not the unpredictable
outcomes of life's ever-ongoing story lines, but its repetitive
facts: fresh frost, a stone plopped in a pond, a waft of hot tar—

common events we're confident will occur, tomorrows
so familiar we can draw them into our minds with calm;
imaginings that may soothe us even further if we further

concentrate the cadences of these everyday experiences
to a single root rhythm in which all—simply for being—
rhymes; a final poem, beyond words, to memorize.

Running Late

Yet Stopping to Look

Summer Stoop Sitting

A bored little girl, chin in hand,
sits on a cool stoop and watches

a building super hose down
the darkening sidewalk then

she glances up as a logo-stamped truck
blocks the café across the street, the

driver grating open its metal flank
for a beer and soda delivery, then

she notes a postal woman, earbuds in,
pushing her cart into a nearby building

while a van gets emptied of pipes
and businessmen on cell phones

stress by and cabs rattle past, all
this adult labor, the listless girl's

face seems to say, as ordained
as passing clouds and breezes

so deepening the weighty
tedium that makes her rise

and turn to slog
discontentedly inside

when her mother appears
in the doorway with a broom

to sweep the stoop
and the girl stops

and snaps alert as if
all these diverse doings

had suddenly formed into
one, foreboding impression

that makes her spin back, once
her mother's sweeping is done,

and plop down to exactly
what she had been doing:

experiencing the sweet, fated,
childhood weight

of nothing
to do.

Alleyways

Three sunlit back alleyways
form an angled intersection
fractured by two parked cars,
overhanging fire escapes,
a dented garbage dumpster,
overgrown weeds, spinning
window fans, air conditioners
thrumming on and off, a mangled
folding chair, a cracked flowerpot,
a slow-weaving cat—all these
and more all threatened
by a wooden water tower
too rotund for its slender stilts.

This jumble of detritus
in stark, wayward contrast
to the buildings' proper stone fronts
and marble lobbies serious people
strut through on serious business
while never imagining
that such old, sober buildings
still struggle with the unmanageable, still
stash evidence of gritty needs, still
manufacture streams of trash
cheap, gaudy, and snarled
as dreams.

Early Snow

The proud Washington Square Arch presents a
statue of the venerable general whose left wrist,

angled against a podium, is the first place on
his person to collect a gentle fall of snow, the

towering, stone-faced, wind-cracked warrior
made suddenly pacific by this soft wristlet.

Iron handrail posts
sprout tiny snowcaps.

Distant shovels, scraping sidewalks, disclose
the rough contours of lightly dusted cement

while the twirling flurry lands
slight and sticky enough to

cling down blades of grass
and along bicycle spokes.

Then the snow drives on
all day to develop into

a soft, white, city-wide
veil.

Around Town

times square

A spring breeze spirits
down worldly

Times Square at night,
its freshness

inviting
a moment

of illuminating
inversion

if you stop,
close your eyes,

and see
with your skin.

*

potted plant

A potted plant tucked
tight to a window

high up a building
presses its large leaves

against the glass, its fronds
crushed and entangled, its

inhibitor invisible, the
distorting effect gaudy.

*

wall

First the fragrance, then—
upon turning the corner—

the sight of a sun struck
brick wall welcoming

a coat of bright whitewash,
the painter's poled roller

reaching high up
the weathered wall

to grant it
the faithful joy

of fresh
forgetting.

By the Natural History Museum

Two little tourist girls
held hands

and watched
their mother

grab
the cell phone

their father was
texting with

and throw it
back at him, the device

bouncing off him
and breaking

apart
on the concrete.

Spring Chill

With the spring day
coursing cool

in the shade,
I turn a street corner

and, struck by sun,
feel

a recollection
start to formulate, not

as an image, or even
as an intangible

muscle memory, but
as from something stored in

bone, a skeleton
memory of my skeleton

childhood-small
and summer-warm,

a memory
radiating out

from marrow
to muscles

and veins
and skin

to return me—
for a full, brimming moment—

to a sweet, long lost
emptiness.

Running Late

Yet Leaving No One Behind

Train Station

One knee set in a wooden wagon, my dad,
as a boy in Maine in the 1930s, would

scoot downhill from the farmhouse
to the local railway station

for no good reason but that things happened there,
and the larger world, steaming with purpose, would

rollick past, headed from elsewhere to elsewhere,
which made his feet feel in nowhere, though occasionally

a train would pause enough for a few elsewhere people
and goods to disembark and disperse so become part of

his nowhere world, though not of his yet lesser world
of chores and chickens and grandparents, the hill back

up a steep, lonely climb to the attic room that held his cot,
a room allowed to him, he knew, from love, yet one

far from the midnight rumbles of the trains that invaded, then
dominated, his steaming-elsewhere, Maine-forsaking dreams.

the notebooks

my mother kept a log / in cheap / pocket notebooks / of the
weekend jaunts / from small town connecticut to new york city /
she made with my father / when they were a young couple with
two young children who / for these special occasions / they
appropriately left home

on their sunday night return / she would consult the scrawled list of
things they did / and expound for my sister and me / on how those
tv game shows had such surprisingly small sets / on how that
hawaii kai restaurant was so fiery and large / and early 1960s new
york / would rise before our innocent / provincial eyes / in all its
neon lit / profligate / sexy / sophistication / our breadwinning
father / on the living room sidelines / still in his suit and knotted
tie / rocking on his heels and beaming

after our mother's death / my sister and i came upon those
swollen / curling notebooks / of sketchy memory prompts that /
while in her own hand / sat sadly flat on the page / for they lacked
the detail and color and gesture / her bubbly amplifications brought
to them

yet she'd saved them / along with playbills to broadway shows
they attended / mostly forgotten flops with discounted tickets /
since those trips / while giddily exciting / were taken pricewise

so the value of the notebooks / was strictly sentimental / and of
course we kept them / but with a nagging feeling of falsity / for
with our mother gone / they were no longer useful as memory
prompts / while to the descendants who won't have known her /
the notebooks' impersonality / will fail to warm them to her once
vivacious reality / a discomforting truth we chose to deny / by
treating the notebooks as telling treasures / evading another of the
telling losses / ever handed down

Mine

I was in the yard working
when I heard, through the
open kitchen window,
my wife tap a spoon shank
on the edge of a cooking pot.

Of course, it was my mother I heard,
as if transported to years ago,
me a boy, playing in the yard, dusk falling,
my father clipping hedges,
my hunger just starting to gnaw.

Then one of my boys ran past crying,
"Mom? Is it dinner yet?"
and I, brought back to the present,
hedge clippers open wide,
knew that that boy—
not a duplicate of me
or owned by anybody—
was, nevertheless, in a living line
of felt continuity,
mine.

setting the watch

it sleeps in a maroon velvet jewelry box / the gold pocket watch
once my grandfather's

during its recent presentation to me / my father / now elderly /
instructed me to wind it each day / to keep it in good repair

which is why it seems asleep / ticking with dreams born
of generational memories

some days / of course / i forget and the watch stops / so when
i remember i simply rewind and reset it / no harm done

then it occurred to me that resetting the time was irrelevant
to the maintenance task / so i no longer bothered with that

but soon i found that no longer bothering with that bothered me /
it was irrational / but i felt somehow disrespectful / so i resumed

the resetting / as if to keep accurate the watch's dream
remembrances / this timekeeper / one i now consider mine

someday to be my sons'

The Wedding Picture

Back in the 1940's, the name big bands—the Glenn Miller,
the Benny Goodman, the Dorsey Brothers—

all played the covered Pier
at Old Orchard Beach, Maine.

From the beach, strolling arm-in-arm with my father,
my mother said she could see the nighttime pier,

strung with lights, swaying from
the jitterbugging bobbysoxers.

Then again, she
was in teenage love.

My teenage father first noticed my mother
in St. Ignatius Church when she looked up

the aisle he was coming down and he saw
those big brown eyes. Soft, needy eyes

that made him—harnessed by the early loss
of his father and early care

for his fragile, melancholy mother—
feel released inside.

For what those lost eyes seemed to long for, he knew,
from experience, he could provide.

In one wedding picture, they stroll, arm-in-arm,
as newlyweds, up that very church aisle,

and if you enter the picture you can almost
smell the flowers, but also salt air; can

hear the recessional organ music,
but also the breaking ocean,

the distant swing band,
the creaking pier.

This black-and-white photo—
crumpled, creased, scratched, torn—

that encodes the remedial, dangerous,
black-and-white love of the young.

Trust

No dream of mine
has been more transparent,
less lost in the clotted symbolism
born of crowded needs: I was bending
toward my son—about four in the dream though
now 23 and headed for graduate school abroad—and
told him—as if time traveling—*Don't ever worry,*
I've seen you as a grown man and you're to be
a wonderful man.

I suppose
I was reminding
myself that he was all grown
up and well beyond worrying about, and
sure enough, when I told my son of this dream he
seemed to look inward—to the grown man he'd become—
with the same look of trust he, as a boy, gave to me in the dream
and he left for his life adventure, both of us believers,
both of us freed.

Born Again

My son now
a father, I'm as mesmerized
by him
as when he was born, for
once again
his face is new, his movements new,
his cradle potential
newly unfolding—
a new life
come into his, he is rendered,
through his fatherly love,
born again.

the reunion

a tall slender woman in a long white skirt-set / face gentle / hair cut
short / camera dangling from around her neck / walks in a group
while holding up a narrow vertical sign like one you'd see at a
political convention announcing that region's delegation

benoit it reads / the name of my father's mother's line / the woman
in white / though taller / a double for eva / my grandmother / and
her four sisters / all now long gone

this photograph / appearing in the new york times / was taken at a
reunion of french families exiled by the acadian dispersal / the
british removal of the french from nova scotia / two-hundred-and-
fifty years ago

all french farmlands were confiscated / thousands died at sea /
some made it back to france / some went to frontier parts of north
america / some to what became louisiana / giving that region its
distinctly cajun style

their gathered descendants / filled plastic bags with nova scotia
earth / their stolen land / to take home from this solemn gathering

one woman / interviewed / spoke her truth and i heard the voice
of eva / who at twenty-three lost her beloved husband to a july 4th
drunken driver / and heard the voice of lena / refusing three offers
of marriage to help her desolated sister raise my then infant father /
heard marie / making her home the heart of our extended family
while privately grieving her own childlessness / heard / even / in
their best moments / the wilder alice and sickly bea

it's a gentle perseverance / the woman said of the descendants'
struggle with the trauma they refused to let destroy their families /
their faith / their hope / their humor / their kindness

a trauma / only through this photograph / i came to know
my ancestors endured

a special resistance she said / her wisdom guiding me / through
bitter tears

Running Late

Yet in a Spell

DJs

Two alternative rock disc jockeys using
handheld mics with the station's call letters
molded in a block above their grip laughed
at each other's rocker inside jokes and
shook their heads at the other's overinformed
antics and argued session dates and players
and releases and split every hair they could
with unabashed dedication to complete-ism
while never meeting eyes, each gazing off to
a different part of the tiny studio, the vital,
crowded, intimate world they created purely
auditory.

Then they signed off and slipped off
their headsets and set down their mics
and inadvertently caught eyes—a connection
both deflected from, each instead rushing out
before the vital, crowded, intimate, incomplete
world of the other could rush in.

The Project

A steelworker
in an orange hard hat
calls down commands
from within a giant square of girders
soon to be unseen, girders
that reveal, for now,
the core geometry
of the building, one
rising like a sculpture
even its artist, once
his metalwork is done, will need
a key to enter.

The Corner

I devote a corner
to a lamp, books, and desk chair
I withdraw to
come evening, a corner
quiet
as the corner
of a boxing ring
between rounds, the hectoring world
unheard, the fighter's focus
lost to the reviving work
done on him—the rub, the balm,
the sting.

the rooming house

the wall between us was so thin / i could hear him pour his tea / in a basement room i rented in a rooming house on beacon street / boston / 1973

garbage cans stood outside my alleyway window / rats / big as cats / waddled past / i picked my mail up from a dark entryway table where / once a week / i left a modest check / cashed by the owner / whom i met only once / the desperate day i'd discovered that the decent apartment i thought i'd secured the spring before / had been let over summer vacation to a fellow music-conservatory student who'd offered to pay more

my tiny room was so overfilled by its stained cot and poor-excuse-for-a-desk / that my friends stopped visiting / if three of us sat down to talk / all our knees touched / not that i could entertain anyway / a single-burner hot plate set atop a microfridge / my complete kitchen / along with a drip-stained corner sink

my neighbor to the south was a young indian man / which was why i figured it was tea he poured / i glimpsed him in the hall / in a dark suit / only once / but i heard / despite my efforts to block them out / all the details of his personal life

the most disconcerting moment was upon his arrival home / silent but for footsteps coming down the hall / silent but for the turning of his poor-excuse-for-a-lock then / upon the closing of his hollow door / a burst of crazed laughter like / as is said of it / i don't know for myself / a hyena's / this weird / cackling laughter was so predictable i took / looking up from my book / *the magic mountain* that year / to miming him / then his jabbering began / thank god in dialect / so became just background noise to join the foraging rats / unless he was feeling especially discontent / in which case the human misery / behind the strangeness of meaning / brought his distress / distressingly home

sometimes he competed with the room to my north / where an
aging / pasty-faced blue-collar worker / tuned his radio to an angry
24-hour call-in talk show / i glimpsed him only once too / meaning
he / the indian / and the owner / all gave me / as if in some vast
rooming-house conspiracy / just one visual shot

most days i was gone / busy at the conservatory / the tiny room just
a crash pad / but sometimes / late at night / i'd lie on my cot /
hemmed in by the dementia of the young indian / and the bitter
resentment / expressed through his radio / of the old / solitary
worker and find / as if all the hours of rehearsals and classes and of
going to concerts and movies and restaurants and jazz clubs with
my friends meant nothing / that i'd been singing a lonely /
wordless blues / loud enough / were anyone listening / to be heard
next door

Four-Way Independence

Try this at home: Sit in a chair
and count out loud to four in
a loop, then start tapping your
right foot on one and two and
your left foot on three—easy
enough—then tap your thigh
with your right hand on one
through four while keeping your
feet the same and once that's
smooth let your left hand join
in on your left thigh tapping
three beats to your right hand's
two—so six at the end of the loop—
and this, for drummers, is routine stuff
but of course when starting out you
choke, each limb wanting to join
its neighbor and proceed in lockstep
so you have to break it down, get
a couple of limbs going before trying
to add the others, work different
combinations of that, repeating and
repeating despite your frustration over
how hard it is to grow into syncing
simple but contradictory parts.

chick

at the end of a dark day / at my mother's wake / i experienced a
discordant hallucination / for by the funeral home door / guests
streaming by him / stood the short / grinning / gum-snapping drum
teacher of my teenage years / chick chicolus

of course it wasn't him / if alive he'd be a creaky antique / not this
sure-footed / hands-on-hips / crowd-parting visage / born of my
exhaustion and grief

but the ghost kept staring at me / reveling as i wrestled with rising
confusion / so finally / admitting derangement / i spoke to it

mr chicolus?

and i should have known / considering the theatrical / spot-lit
entrance he'd just made / that it actually was him

ninety-four years old / it turned out / and looking no different / i
swear / than when i biked to his house for lessons on his ancient
drums / his bass drum big as a washing machine tub / museum
pieces / really / from his youthful career as a vaudeville-style
drummer

chick strode up and shook my hand / without a word about our
loss / as he was too pumped by his effect on me for such
formalities / a condition i stoked by stepping away from the
receiving line / calling over my two grown sons / and chirping to
them / like a distractible thirteen-year-old / an introduction

to this expanded audience / chick talked about his teaching days /
how he'd take four drum students to residential homes for
children / with special needs / who would clap along / with
perfection / to our purely rhythmic routine / then he talked of the
acts he played for way back when / the singers / dancers / jugglers /

and comedians he'd get laughs for / with his bottomless bag of
sound effects / i remembered their signed / glossy head shots /
mounted in his basement drum studio / photos hopelessly dated
and corny / to a youngster yearning to inhabit the cool precincts of
jazz

then even my dad and my sister / as they couldn't help but notice /
came over / the wake a temporary house party / with chick at the
center / acting out a stream of jokes and stories / while snapping
his ever-present gum

then at the top of his game / he shook our hands and headed out /
we all but breaking into applause on his waving exit / he never
having paid his respects to my mother / who would have smiled
like the fan of his she was / and approved / for she knew his only
seemingly / cruel code

the show must go on

Running Late

Yet Watching Others

In Study

A small boy
standing under an awning
beside his dad and toddler-sister
with his hands in his pockets
looking out to the rain

seems
in deep study of
standing under an awning
with your hands in your pockets
looking out to the rain;

seems in acquisition
of another angle—
this one calm and patient—
from which to witness
long, changeable days.

Strollers

Some moms but mostly babysitters
fill the concrete steps as they wait
for their little preschoolers, empty
strollers parked below and beside
the rising stair wall, skeletal vehicles
left in their own little lot, a rising
breeze gently rolling then twirling
the strollers backward until sudden
crosswinds make them collide like
bumper cars and though none of the
moms or babysitters notice—they're
busy greeting the children and their
teachers—no stroller falls or escapes
as they seem too absorbed in the sheer
fun of knocking about and tangling up,
as if through all the hours of hauling
their charges—imprinting their shapes
and stains and smells—the strollers had
drawn in the essence of each child, had
become shadow-kids, kids—with all
the adults preoccupied—wildly alive.

Playgroup

A dozen or so schoolgirls
of mixed age and size, all
wearing puffy nylon jackets
and colorful woolen hats, sit
in a circle right on the cold
playground tar and listen
to a teacher explain the rules
of a game they seem about to
play—something to do with
hoops; a teacher whose own
winter wear matches that of
her charges, making her seem
like a more grown version of
them—or they, perhaps, past
versions of her: bygone selves
she didn't discard but distilled
and retained and harmonized,
so fully present and listening,
enrapt, on this cold winter day,
to what's coming next.

Bus Driver

A yellow school bus parked
at the curb in the rain stands
empty of students, its stop signs
tucked in, the old driver walking
down the aisle, his head turning
side to side to check each row for
forgotten backpacks, stray books,
dropped electronics, pens underfoot—
and most of all for sleeping kids.

But he finds nothing so lumbers
back to the driver's seat and plops
down with a sigh—this weathered
man with a drooping moustache—
I can nearly hear from outside, set
to move on yet somehow unable to, instead
checking the mirrors, readjusting the seat—
then closing his eyes and clenching
the steering wheel, the bus the shell,
it suddenly seems, of his own childhood,
a childhood so hollowed by hard years
that a search of it would yield no
forgotten, discarded, or sleeping
dream he could use to drive himself
on.

Waiters

Two Indian waiters in snug tuxedos
sit on steps a few doors down from

their deserted restaurant—I just passed it—
sharing a smoke and quiet talk, talk that could

be about the coming end of their run there,
about what other jobs might appear, about

whom they should call or visit:
a strategy session.

Yet so spare and emphatic is their conversation,
its silences inhabited by blue clouds of smoke,

that between their middle-aged declarations
of determination they each may be feeling

an unsparing circle closing in; feeling the
dread approach of the night they fear most:

the night they take their tuxedos off and
never have cause to put them back on—

no more trips to the dry cleaners, no more
updating the bow tie; instead, back to wearing

the loose, patterned shirtsleeves of cab drivers
pulling 12-hour shifts spelled only when parked

to eat curry out of plastic containers from the Bengali deli;
hours logged making drop-offs at trendy, Pan-Asian restaurants

whose young, stylishly dressed doormen—the age of
their own sons?—come right to the cab to open then—

after the fares step out—turn away while
slamming the door.

Burials

The night she buried
her husband—

they were both thirty-three—
Alison

took his twin brother
to bed in a crazed, ghoulish

attempt to allay
her desolating grief.

Three years later, she lay dying
of ovarian cancer.

"Just punishment," she said, unjustly,
"For what I did that night."

Then she crossed and clenched,
beneath the hospital sheets,

her once
beautiful legs.

*

Just off a tour of duty in Vietnam, Billy took a job loading
information—the numbing name and address labels that

drove a local distribution company—
into its new, room-sized computer.

Not yet drafted for the War but waiting for notice,
I held the job of hauling file card drawers to Billy

then, once he'd punched them in, returning them
to the slotted cabinets that became their mausoleums.

The computer was sealed in its own plate-glass room,
those early models famously temperamental.

At lunch in the cafeteria, Billy told stories of how a
mere speck of dust, dead fly, or badly timed sneeze

had gummed-up some state-of-the-art but
fragile computer he once knew.

He never talked about Vietnam, despite my worried questions.
Just said that it was okay.

Except for the stink of jungle mud, which he said would
hang on his uniform, infiltrate his pack, cling to his hair.

Sometimes, he once confided, he could still
smell it on his skin.

Then he stood up, wiped the crumbs away, washed
his hands, brushed his teeth, splashed his face and—

snapping latex gloves and a surgical mask on—
returned to the dry, odorless, temperature

controlled room that held
room for one.

*

Red, at nine, didn't know
until his hands knew

then he knew
how the machinery worked,

why a job of carpentry fit,
what each tangled electrical wire did.

His hands were quick, inquisitive, appreciative
of a complexity

he could never have spoken
or written of.

Our teachers, back then, said he was dumb
and Red, folding his hands on his desk

as ordered,
believed them.

Park Bench

What he was saying
to himself
he kept silent, this
young, heavyset man
sitting elbows to knees
on a park bench, his black
T-shirt and pants and greasy hair
studded with dried grass, presumably
from having slept on the nearby slope; grass
he didn't bother to brush off; grass
so embedded it looked like something
emitted: a dream
made manifest, overnight, in coded
text, the young man himself—
lips moving inaudibly—
lost in translation.

Running Late

Yet Having To Wade

After Loss

the days
nest—

precariously—

like empty
bowls.

*

A gold cigarette
butt, twisted

candy wrapper, discarded
plastic spoon, and dark,

flattened disk of gum
surround a blade

of grass growing
from a broken sidewalk,

the sprig seeming
a humble

probe of life
after

devastation, kindred spirit
to the tender

fleck of green
floating

on the quiet
pond in the spoon.

Symptoms

who you know yourself as

is what is at risk

when your body feels

stark fear that comes

not from outer threat to your body

but from what your body senses inwardly

which is that it is losing you and knows

it is nothing

you betraying lover

without you

Jingle

I lean my elbows,
idly, on
an uneven café table
and everything
jingles—flatware
chinking, sliding saucer
tinkling ice cubes in a glass that
clinks a sugar dispenser—and I'm
awoken from
my sketchy, troubled, already-
vanished reverie of elsewhere,
my raised elbows
resettling—and resettling me to—
the durable
flatware, glass, saucer.

Disturbances

A night
dark as the sleep that eludes me.

A lone
streetlamp—I rise to see—slanted with rain.

Rushing
tire treads creasing the street's black wetness.

Dampness
weighting the wrangled sheets I wade back into.

Disturbances
so distinct, lush, and insistent

they seed a drizzly, then
finally

drenching
rainfall of dreams.

Running Late

Yet Taking the Garden Path

Early Spring

Snowfall
this enchanting

falls from clouds,
it seems, dissolving

then reforming:
heaven

held
earthbound.

*

Their southern slants
bared of snow

while their northern slopes
hold white,

these gentle hills
roll perfectly

poised
between seasons—

still
change itself.

*

With the spring-fed lake
spring-cleaned

of algae, bright
schools of minnows

appear above dark predators—
so clear is this water—predators

who break surface
when they must, the spared

minnows scattering and re-gathering
as they must,

the lake water
restoring,

as it must, to deep
calm.

Spring Snow

Spring snow
slackens from the sidewalk
on this day of rain, though
not from the old, gated, padlocked
cemetery, its crisp white cover still
spread as if change
on the far side of the wrought-iron fence
moves more slowly, time
stalled by the stillness
of the graves, yesterday itself held
captive to the cold
pull of yesterdays already
abiding there.

Clouds

Drifting with adagio drama,
the light, lofty clouds

sketch the sky with wishes:
with cloud

bison, horses, faces
of gods.

*

This low pewter sky
returns the soft days

when I'd see in
such a cover

a reflection
of the mysteries

that clouded
my wondering childhood;

clouds that seemed,
back then,

certain to clear;
then, come midlife, seemed

certain to lower;
then finally

came simply
to reflect

my found
reverence

for the
certain light

pewter skies
throw.

Heat Lightning

We felt alone
at the top of the world
though it was just a high stretch
of the relatively runty Berkshire mountains
that we were driving late one summer night, the road
deserted but for us, the black sky a low, intimate presence

suddenly lit
by a southern flash
of heat lightning that made
not a sound, an absence that didn't
square with something so dramatic, with this radiance
roundly blasting the countryside, the humped mountains—

silhouetted—made
gigantic, the pointed pines
and rugged valleys below exposed;
then a companion flash came from the north,
then the western and eastern skies got involved, all combining to
create a cacophony of silent flares, the beautifully stark landscape

alive with us
the only witnesses
to this overlapping conversation
ranged beyond our hearing; a discussion that
even if we could hear it we wouldn't fathom; yet one that,
as we drove along—each other lit too—spoke of thunderous joy.

Sunset

The sun, already
set behind our mountain,
casts us into shadow while keeping
the mountain across the valley in daylight,

the evening we now
inhabit made to seem a past
concurrent with a luminous present
beyond which yet higher mountains rise

in a bright, if
hazy, future, this snapshot of
all time as one time an impression
we savor until the sun, as it must, fully sets.

The Ocean

The calm blue ocean
out the open cottage door presents
a great simplicity, makes the busy interior—the kitchen
pots and pans, the space heaters, even the rockers on the porch—

seem too precious, too
formed to fit us, too devoted to tending
to everyday needs; and while the great ocean
cannot offer one simple answer it does ask one simple question

we find ourselves ever
unable to answer—unless you count
simple devotion to all that has offered devotion
through our long, complicated, weathering years—starting with

these dinged pots and pans, these balky space heaters,
these salt-scraped rockers on the porch
that hold us
still.

About the Author

Mark Belair's poems have appeared in *Harvard Review, Michigan Quarterly Review,* and *Poetry East* among other journals. His previous collections include *Watching Ourselves; Breathing Room; Night Watch; While We're Waiting;* and *Walk With Me.*

Please visit www.markbelair.com

Made in the USA
Coppell, TX
19 November 2019